Garden Walk

For children learning
to love reading.

First Edition
27 26 25 24 23   5 4 3 2 1

Copyright © 2023 Virginia Brimhall Snow

Published by Gibbs Smith
P.O. Box 667 Layton, Utah 84041
1.800.835.4993 orders
www.gibbs-smith.com

Manufactured in China in September 2022 by Toppan.

Gibbs Smith books are printed on either recycled, 100%post-consumer waste, FSC-certified papers or on paper produced from a 100% certified sustainable forest/controlled wood source.

Library of Congress Control Number: 2022940724
ISBN: 978-1-4236-6252-5

Garden Walk

VIRGINIA BRIMHALL SNOW

Gibbs Smith

day lily

Grammy and I walked through her garden today.

pine

We explored the woods
where I like to play.

aspen

robin

She pushed the swing, hung from a branch up so high,
and I giggled with glee as my feet touched the sky.

"Look at me, little birdies, come watch me fly!"

marigold

butterfly

We showered thirsty flowers
with our garden hose.

I watched as a butterfly
fluttered right past my nose.

black-eyed Susan

ladybug

"Grammy, there are red bugs chomping on this flower!"

"Ladybugs eat pests," she said. "It's their superpower."

raspberries

pear

From prickly bushes
I picked juicy berries.

I nibbled a few—
there were too many to carry.

tomato

I found ripe tomatoes
a real yummy treat,

while Grammy picked
green beans for us to eat.

green beans

carrots

bunny

"Let's dig a few carrots
and pull out some weeds.

They take light and water
that our veggies will need."

gladiola

"Oh, look there's a hummingbird darting over there."

I watched it sip nectar, hovering right in the air.

hummingbird

We picked peppers and cucumbers,
but the pumpkins weren't ready.

Then the dog dashed to meet us.
"Watch out for me, Freddie!"

llama

pumpkin.

dragonfly

I threw his ball hard,
and Freddie ran really fast

all 'round the yard,
with dragonflies zipping past.

Freddie

wasp

"Can I play in the clubhouse?
Are the wasp nests all gone?"

peach

"It's safe now," called Grammy,
as she rested on the lawn.

scrub
jay

red maple

A squirrel raced 'cross the
grass between Grammy and me,

stole seeds from the birds,
then zoomed up the tree.

chicken

I joined in the chase,
because it looked so much fun,

apple

then played in the garden
'til the morning was done.

oak

deer

We spread out a blanket in the shade of the tree.

And I munched on some lunch while Grammy read to me.

fun food

SMILING SANDWICH

Peanut butter
Honey, jam, or jelly
Bread (1 slice per serving)
Raspberries or blackberries
Apple slices

To make an open-face sandwich, spread peanut butter and honey, jam, or jelly on 1 slice of bread. Then place berries for eyes and an apple slice for the mouth to make your smiling sandwich.

CAPRESE KABOBS

Cherry or grape tomatoes
Basil leaves
Mozzarella cheese sticks, cut into pieces
Olives
Toothpicks
Balsamic vinaigrette salad dressing (optional)

Put the ingredients above the salad dressing on a toothpick in the order listed to make little kabobs. Place the kabobs on a plate and drizzle salad dressing over them, if desired.

CUP OF VEGGIES

Ranch salad dressing
Mug or short clear plastic cup
Baby carrots or carrot sticks
Celery sticks
Fresh green beans, snapped
Green, yellow, orange, or red pepper sticks, sliced

Put as much salad dressing as desired in the bottom of a mug or cup. Fill the cup with veggies, standing them on their ends in the dressing.

ANTS ON A LOG

Celery sticks
Peanut butter
Raisins

Fill the groove in the celery stick with peanut butter. Make a line of raisins down the center of the peanut butter.